GOD CREATED ME!

Illustrated by Nikki Boetger

warner press KiDS

305800215454

In the beginning, God created a beautiful world.

And God saw that it was good. GENESIS 1:12 (NIV)

God put fish in the water and birds in the sky.

Let the water teem with living creatures, and let birds fly above.

GENESIS 1:20 (NIV)

Then God made all kinds of animals.

God said, "Let the land produce living creatures." GENESIS 1:24 (NIV)

Finally, God created a man. His name was Adam.

The LORD God formed a man from the dust. GENESIS 2:7 (NIV)

God created a woman too. Adam named her Eve.

Then the LORD God made a woman. GENESIS 2:22 (NIV)

The Bible says God made people in His image.
That means boys and girls too!

Male and female he created them. GENESIS 1:27 (NIV)

God gave each person a body.
Bodies come in different shapes and sizes.

Honor God with your bodies. 1 CORINTHIANS 6:20 (NIV)

God used many beautiful colors for our skin.

I am . . . wonderfully made. PSALM 139:14 (NIV)

God created our eyes in different shapes and colors.

My eyes are ever on the LORD. PSALM 25:15 (NIV)

God had fun making hair straight, curly, and wavy. On some heads, God put no hair at all!

The very hairs of your head are all numbered. MATTHEW 10:30 (NIV)

God made each person exactly right!

God created mankind in his own image. GENESIS 1:27 (NIV)

We can think and talk. We can learn new things.

Learn to do right. ISAIAH 1:17 (NIV)

We can paint, sing, or dance.
We can even play instruments and do gymnastics!

We have different gifts. ROMANS 12:6 (NIV)

We can love others and be kind.

Love one another. 1 JOHN 4:7 (NIV)

God created you, and He loves you just the way you are. You are the best YOU ever!